SURPRISE PAPER TEARING TALKS

NUMBER 9

ARNOLD CARL WESTPHAL

"THE CHILDRENS' SHEPHERD"

AUTHOR

Gospel Surprise Visual Aids
Junior Surprise Object Talks
Visual Evangels Surprise Pack
Visual Evangelettes
Gospel Surprise Objectalks
Eye-Gate Surprise Gospel Lessons
Handi-Pack Gospel Object Lessons
Gospel Surprise Object Kit
Magic Climax Visual Aids
Chemic-Color Gospel Lessons
ETC.

VISUAL EVANGELS PUBLISHERS 1401 Ohio Street

MICHIGAN CITY, INDIANA

PREFACE

Solomon said there is nothing new under the sun, but everything conceivable has been used in object lessons to illustrate Bible truth.

Paper tearing is not a new approach to the technique of teaching and this NUMBER 9 manual, added to the 8 this author has previously devised, written and published will be the completion of ninety surprise paper tears implemented to reveal Bible truth. It is hoped that the ideas will serve as an oasis in the desert of this neglected field.

The lessons cannot improve or renovate the gospel but they are offered as mediums to simplify the Good News. An advertiser said, "We cannot improve our product so we improved the container in which it comes."

Careful study of the lessons will assure the worker that a sincere effort has been made to more fully reveal the Christ of the Cross. In these darkest days of church life he humbly offers the tool, sharpened by an unfailing faith that the darkest darkness cannot put out the flickering light of the smallest candle. These tiny lessons for the tiny people may be as timeless as the eternity they are signposts to.

INTRODUCTION

This is not a book of words but of ideas which were designed to satiate the hungry appetites of workers among children.

Workers are always on the loose, searching for unusual approaches to young and hungry hearts, superimposed by curious minds.

The sermonic content is not written in the language of the child, but with the hope that the worker will "originalize" and suit the lesson in the language that will suit the variety of ages that filter into the childrens' services.

This is the age of graded departments, classes and lessons, but no method has yet been devised to grade the soul. Every child of whatever age, lacks spiritual calories and his soul will not become obese readily.

There are two parts to each lesson, the handwork and the homework. The handwork is the preparation of the object and the homework is the preparation for teaching the truth the object is to amplify. Both require diligent and prayerful effort on the part of the worker.

This author used the tape and mirror method successfully. He watched himself give the lesson as he recorded what he said. Then he looked and listened with horror at his "masterpiece." Now he revised the inept and misplaced illustrations and Scriptures that seemed far-fetched and performed surgery on wordiness and used the dismembered ragged remains as a potent lesson, usually leaving an intrigued audience.

FIRST PRINTING 1976

ISBN 0-915398-08-7

PRINTED IN U.S.A

TABLE OF CONTENTS

1. "HAPPY BIRTHDAY AMERICA" 10
2. THE KISSING GATE 14
3. A WORLD WITHOUT WINDOWS 19
4. LITTLE IS MUCH WHEN GOD IS IN IT 25
5. BIBLE BALLS AND CHAINS 30
6. BEGINNING AT THE BEGINNING 35
7. ACROBATIC CHRISTIANS 40
8. BIRTHDAY SHOES 45
9. THE MISER'S BASKET 50
10. SAFE AT LAST 56

CHAPTER 1

"HAPPY BIRTHDAY" AMERICA

And now they seek a better country; that is
an heavenly" (Heb. 11:16).

PART 1

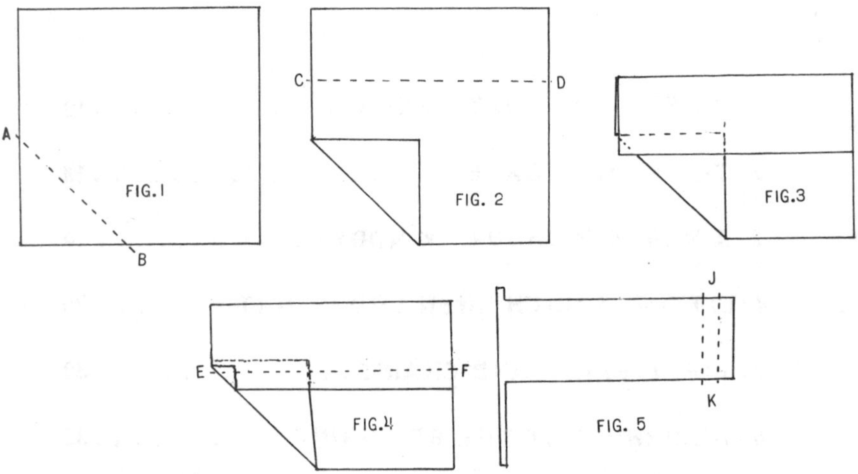

PART 2

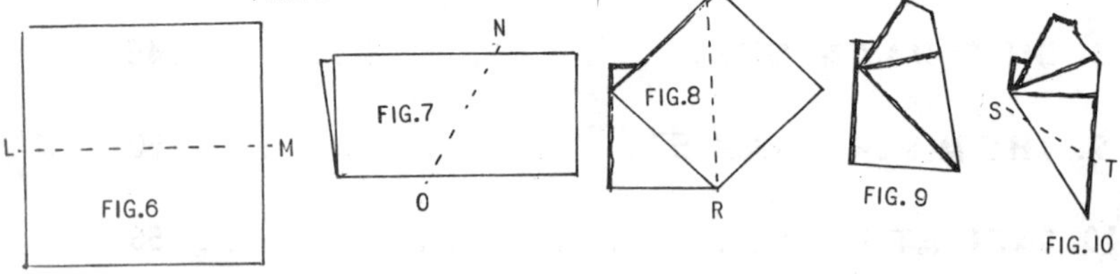

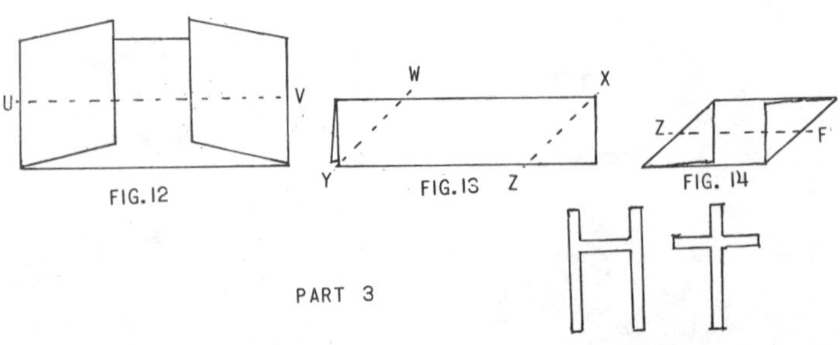

PROPERTY

Three Sheets of paper in the following sizes - 12 X 12 inches, 6 X 6 inches and 3 X 9 inches or proportionate sizes to suit the auditorium size.

PREPARATION

Note that the drawing has parts 1,2 and 3. Prefold Fig. 1 on line AB and Fig. 2 on line CD to make Fig. 3. Prefold the small corner at point E firmly against the sheet. Then unfold.

In Part 2, prefold the 6 X 6 sheet (Fig. 6) on line LM. Then fold on line ON and again on line PR to Fig. 9. Fold the remaining corner of Fig. 9 to make Fig. 10. Unfold. In Part 3 take the 3 X 9 sheet and prefold ends almost to the center as in Fig. 12. Now prefold on line UV. Fold corners over all the previous folds as in Figs. 13 and 14. Unfold and you are ready for the lesson.

PROCEDURE

Fold Fig. 1 to Fig. 4 and cut on line EF. After unfolding the flag, cut a couple of stripes from the end on lines JK of Fig. 5. Bisect Fig. 6 with a fold to make Fig. 7. Fold Fig. 7 on line ON and again on line PR. Cut on line ST of Fig. 10 and unfold a star.

In Part 3 fold Fig. 12 as shown, to Fig. 14. Cut on line ZF of Fig. 14 and unfold the letter H and a cross.

PRESENTATION

The word Flag is mentioned in the Bible only four times, and always as a growing weed-like plant in a swamp. It was among such flags that the baby Moses was hidden in a home-made basket of bulrushes. (Ex. 2:3).

A flag like we are going to talk about was called a STANDARD in the Bible. It served the same purpose our Betsy Ross flag does today. When Moses was commanded to number or count the people he divided them into tribes. Each tribe was separated as a group and each had a standard or flag. The flag was set in the center of the camp or at headquarters which was the command post.

THE LANDING OF THE PILGRIM PIONEERS

Now about our flag, sometimes called THE STARS AND STRIPES. Our forefathers left England to become an independent nation. They sought a better country. They sailed the long voyage on the Mayflower and landed at Plymouth, Mass. in 1620. They stepped ashore on a big rock that is visited by many vacationing tourists. It is called Plymouth Rock. For the next 150 years they fought with Indians and were in trouble with England. They organized themselves into groups which were called "colonies." Then on July 4, 1776 the leaders signed what they called THE DECLARATION OF INDEPENDENCE and this became the official separation from England and has since been celebrated as the birthday of the United States.

THE BETSY ROSS FLAG

There had been a continuous war between the King's English Red Coats and the patriots of the new nation, but as yet there was no flag or standard for the new nation.

Betsy Ross was a 24 year old widow and one of 17 children. She lived in Philadelpia. It was she who set out to make a flag. (Fold Fig. 1 as shown and cut on line EF of Fig. 4). This is the way the flag looked. (show flag). But Betsy didn't want just a white flag for this is the sign of surrender to the enemy. She had seen so many soldiers die in the War for Independence and so much bloodshed, she thought there should be some red in the flag. She cut strips from the cloth and dyed them red and sewed them on the flag. (Cut strips at line JK Fig. 5). But the flag still looked plain and unfinished.

THE STARS ADDED TO THE STRIPES

Doubtless she had heard criticisms that the new government was disloyal to its mother country, England, so she dyed another piece of cloth blue and sewed it on the upper left hand corner to signify true blue loyalty to the new country and its leaders. But then the blue field looked bare. (Fold Fig. 6 of Part 2 to Fig. 10 and cut on line ST and show a star).

THE COMPLETED FLAG

When the flag was finally finished it had three colors, red, white and blue, 13 stripes and 13 stars to represent the 13 colonies. The stars were sewed on in the form of a circle. Some of the stripes were long and some short. This signified that loyalty would assure long life and disloyalty would breed a short life for the colonies.

THE BIBLE PATRIARCHS

I have shown you how the flag was made, so now let's go from the Pilgrim Patriots to the Bible Patriarchs. Many years before the Mayflower and the Pilgrims and the Declaration of Independence and the Fourth of July Celebrations, the Bible Patriarchs also looked for a better country. It is mentioned in Hebrews 11:16. There was Noah, Abraham, Isaac, Jacob, Joseph, Moses, Gideon, Barak, David and many others. Just as our forefathers desired a better country and became Pilgrim pioneers, so the patriarchs of old looked for a city whose builder and maker was God. The verse says, "But now they desire a better country, that is an heavenly . . . and God prepared for them a city".

THE BETTER COUNTRY

(Fold the 3 X 9 sheet of Part 3 to Fig. 13. Cut on line ZF and unfold the letter H and the cross). What kind of a country did they seek? A HEAVENLY country. (Show H). How can you come to that better country? By a single, simple, sure, straight road that has only one crossroad. It is by way of the cross. (Show cross).

HOW TO GET THERE

The cross has four points pointing down, up and out. The lower point goes down to the earth or world for which Jesus died. The top points you to heaven and the arms that reach out are like an invitation to come, come, come. And whosoever will may come.

CHAPTER 2

THE KISSING GATE

"But when he was yet a far way off, his father saw him and had compassion, and ran and fell on his neck and kissed him."

(Luke 15:20)

PROPERTY

A sheet of newsprint, 6 X 9 inches in size, scissors.

PREPARATION

Prefold Fig. 1 into three equal panels on lines AB and CD, and Fig. 2 on line EF. Pencil lightly the shape of a half head as on Fig. 3, line GH. Unfold and you are ready to proceed with the lesson.

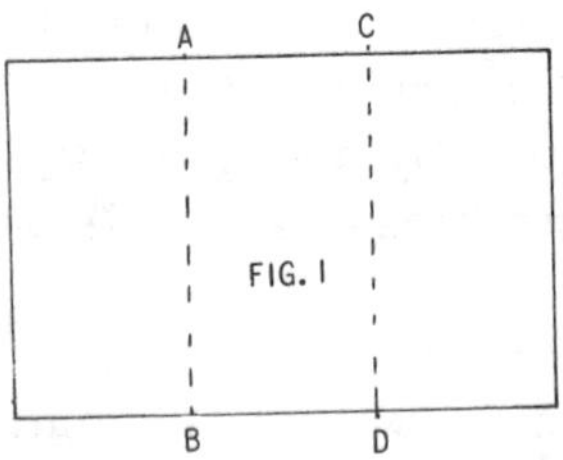

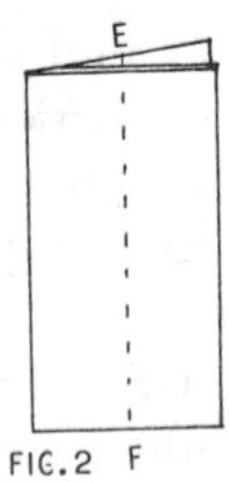

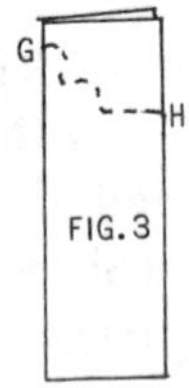

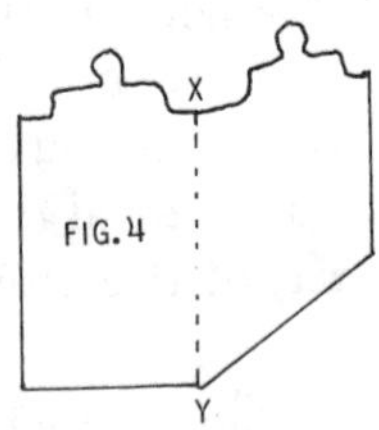

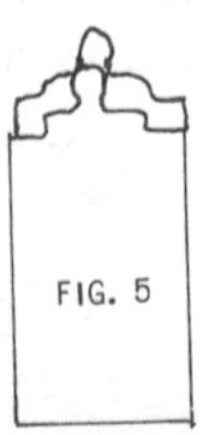

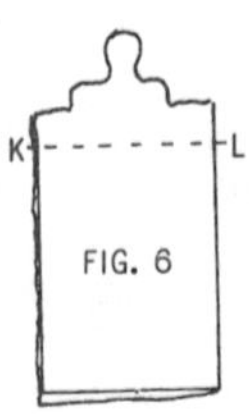

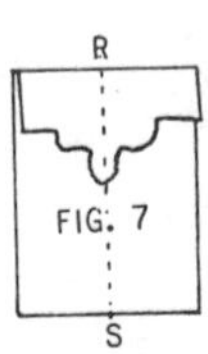

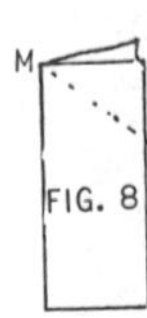

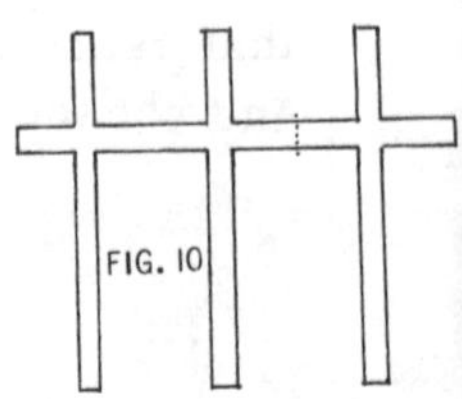

PROCEDURE

During the lesson, fold Fig. 1 to Fig. 3 and cut on line GH. Unfold to Fig. 4, keeping one panel concealed. Fold Fig. 4 on line XY so it appears two faces are kissing. (Fig. 5). Then fold Fig. 6 with three panels folded, on line KL. Fold Fig 7 on line RS. Fold corner of Fig. 8 on line MN. Cut Fig. 9 on line OP near hinged side and show three crosses. Tear off one cross and fold the other two facing each other.

PRESENTATION

In the Bible days, many cities had walls surrounding them. This was true of Jerusalem. There were many gates and each gate had a name. There was the Sheep gate, the Fish gate, the Market gate, the Golden gate, the Water Gate, the East gate and the Gate Beautiful. There was also a small gate built into a large gate and it was called "The Needle's Eye." The large gate was for camels and the small gate was for people. Aside from the gates in Jerusalem, the Bible mentions many other gates, like the gate of heaven, the gates of hell, the gate of death, the gate of the grave, the wide gate, the strait or narrow gate, the gate of praise, etc.

You may never go through all of these gates, but I hope you will make plans to go through the Gates of Pearl that are in the City of God, which is heaven. (Rev. 21:21).

A CHURCH YARD KISSING GATE

I am going to make a Kissing Gate for you. Such a gate was found in a small village called, "Smarden" in Kent, England, near London.

In the village there was a church and a church-yard with a fence around it. To enter the yard, you came down a flagstone walk to a gate. This was called "The Kissing Gate." The gate worked something like this -

(Fold Fig. 1 to Fig. 3 and cut on penciled line, and show how gate swings). There were two gates side by side, one for the boy and the other for the girl. As they opened the gate, as they walked side by side, the gates swung into the church-yard and the lips of the boy and girl met, so the gate was called "The Kissing Gare.".

If we had more gates like that more young people would be in church.

A WILDERNESS KISSING GATE

Let me tell you about the twin brothers, Jacob and Esau. They had become enemies because Jacob had wronged Esau. Each had gone his own way for many years, but one night God touched Jacob's heart as well as his leg. Jacob became lame and now his heart was softened toward his brother. He knew he must make things right with Esau. He gathered together many gifts to give Esau as a peace offering. Then they met in the wilderness. Jacob was so sorry for his sin against his twin brother, but his brother was willing to forgive him, after all their years of separation. When they saw each other, they met as though there was a kissing gate (Gen. 31:4).

A BARN YARD KISSING GATE

A wilfull son left home in anger because his father and mother did not always let him have his way. He was nicknamed THE PRODIGAL SON. The story of his break with his folks is in the 15th chapter of Luke. He went to the Far Country and there joined the wrong crowd. He spent all of his money and soon was ragged, homeless, hopeless and helpless and hungry. He had found that the devil is a poor paymaster. He thought of his lovely home. Finally he decided to go back and ask forgiveness of his father.

Parents are always glad to see their children, no matter what they have done or how much trouble they have caused them. When this disobedient son returned, it was like the father and son were meeting at a kissing gate in the barnyard. (Luke 15:20). The father was willing and ready to forgive and restore the son to his full rights as a son. He not only gave him a kiss, but also a robe, shoes, a ring and a feast.

A CHURCH AISLE KISSING GATE

Usually when you go to church, greetings are exchanged between friends and fellow Christians, but it has not always been by shaking hands as it is today. Instead, they kissed one another. The men kissed the men and the women kissed the women. It was as if there was a kissing gate in the church aisles. This was in keeping with the Bible, for God had said, "Greet one another with a holy kiss." (Rom. 16:16).

A GETHSEMANE KISSING GATE

Kisses are usually given where there is love, but this is not always true. There was a kiss in the Garden of Gethsemane by a false follower of the Lord Jesus. His name was Judas. He had been paid thirty pieces of silver, the price of a slave. For this money he was to kiss the Lord Jesus to identify him as the one the mob was to arrest. Jesus had claimed that he was the Son of God, and many other things which they held against him and for which they intended to put him to death. (Matth. 26:48-49). "Now he that betrayed him gave them a sign, saying, Whomsoever I shall kiss, that same is he, hold him fast, and forthwith he came to Jesus and said, Hail,Master, and kissed him" (Matth. 27:3-5). So the kiss in the Garden was not one of love, but of betrayal.

A GOLGOTHA KISSING GATE

There is one more Kissing Gate. It is on a hill near Jerusalem.It is called "Golgotha" and is also known as "Mount Calvary."

(Fold Fig. 6 on line KL and Fig. 7 on line RS. Fold down the corner of Fig. 8 on line MN. Cut on line OP of Fig. 9. Unfold and show three crosses).

Jesus was crucified with two others so there were three crosses. Jesus may have been pinned to the middle cross. The other two crosses had criminals on them. During the hours of their suffering, each of these two criminals could have done as you will do today, to choose Jesus or to turn him aside. They were in a circle of death and decision. (Hold crosses in a circle by joining the outer arms).

A VALLEY OF DECISION KISSING GATE

One criminal decided he would die as he had lived, and he mocked Jesus. The other decided he would go through the Calvary Kissing Gate, so he begged Jesus to have mercy on him and then claimed him as his Savior by praying, "Lord, remember me when thou comest into thy kingdom"(Luke 23:39-43). Jesus could not give him a kiss on the lips, but he gave him a heart kiss as he assured him, "Today shalt thou be with me in Paradise."

If you go through the Calvary Kissing Gate now, you you will next go through the Gate of Praise. Then, when you come to the gates of death and the grave, you will come joyfully to the gates of Pearl in the walls of jasper. These are the Pearly Gates (Rev. 21:21).

A kiss on the cheek may be a mere kiss of approval, but a kiss on the lips is one of affection. If you come just to Sunday School and once in a while to church, you are just giving Jesus a peck on the cheek, showing you approve him. He wants more than that. He wants true love shown by your loyalty to him daily, ever and always.

CHAPTER 3

A WORLD WITHOUT WINDOWS

" . . . and men loved darkness rather than light because their deeds were evil."

(John 3:19)

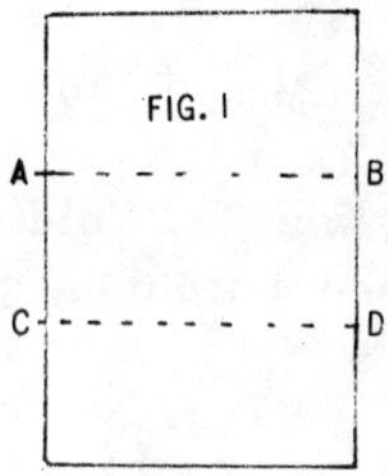

FIG. 1

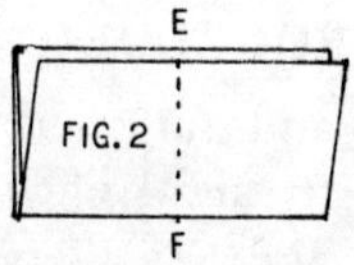

FIG. 2

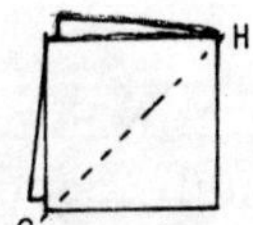

FIG. 3

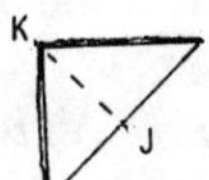

FIG. 4

FIG. 5

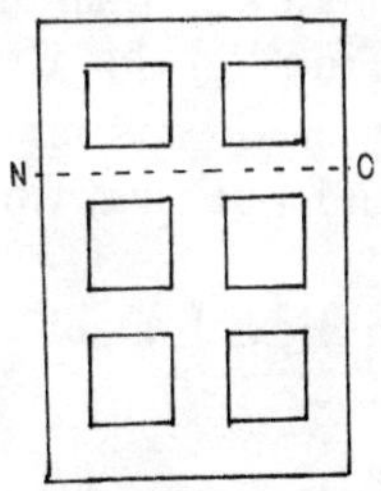

FIG. 6

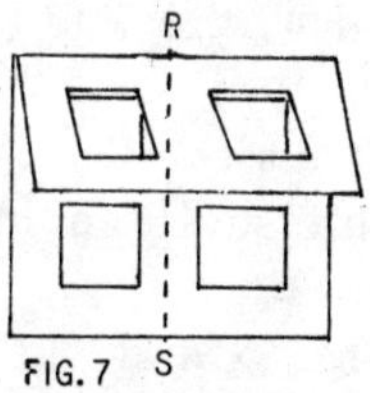

FIG. 7

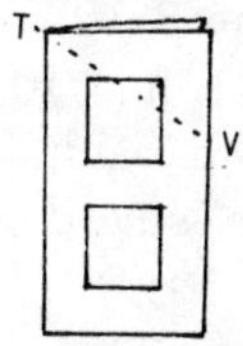

FIG. 8

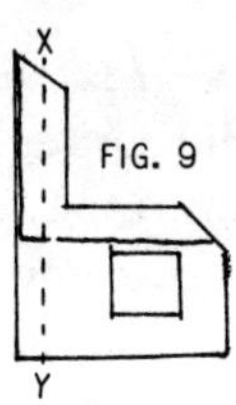

FIG. 9

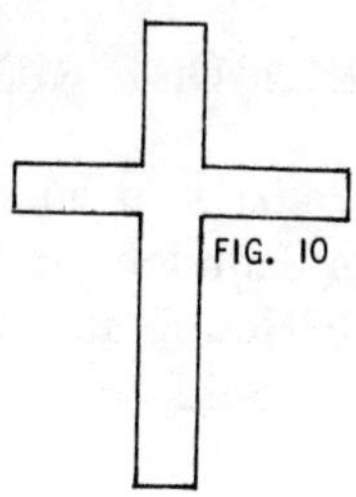
FIG. 10

PROPERTY

A piece of newsprint or other lightweight paper 8 X 12 inches in size or larger in proportionate size, and scissors.

PREPARATION

Prefold Fig. 1 on lines AB and CD and Fig. 2 on line EF to make Fig. 3. Prefold Fig. 3 on line GH to make Fig. 4. Prefold Fig. 4 on line JK. Pencil mark Fig. 5 on line LM. Unfold, beginning the lesson with Fig. 1.

PROCEDURE

Fold Fig. 1 to Fig. 5 and cut on line LM and show Fig. 6, a French style door with six lights. As a lesson climax, fold Fig. 6 on line NO and Fig. 7 on line RS. Fold Fig. 8 on line TV and cut on line XY and unfold a cross.

PRESENTATION

Jesus had many titles. He said, "I am the Light of the world" (John 8:12), I am the Way (John 14:6), I am the Good Shepherd (John 10:11), I am the Vine "(John 15:5).

One day he said, "I am the Door, by me if any man enter, he shall be saved and shall go in and out and find pasture" (John 10:9).

(Fold Fig. 1 to Fig. 5 and cut on line LM and unfold a door).

ONLY ONE RIGHT DOOR

Suppose you wanted to enter a great building like Westminster Abbey in London or Edinborough Castle in Scotland or the White House in Washington, D.C. After finding the building you would look for the door, the RIGHT door. There might be many doors, like the side door, the back door, the kitchen door, the laundry door. You would need to find the right door, the main door, the only door through which you would be permitted to enter unless you were the cook or the washer-woman on the President or King.

WHAT A DOOR IS FOR

A door is for going in and out. Jesus mentioned this two-fold purpose. He said, "I am the door. If any of you come through this door you will be saved, and when you go out through this door you will find food or pasture for your growth." From the very beginning of time, God put doors before his people.

WHAT A WINDOW IS FOR

(Fold to Fig. 5 and cut on line LM). Notice there are six windows in this door. Windows are put in a house or door to let the light in.

God has tried to let the light shine in through these six windows through all the years that have passed. Each of these six windows is for a different way in which he has let the light shine in, but each time somebody has pulled the shade down. So we live in a dark world.

THE INEXCUSABLE FALL OF ADAM AND EVE

In creation God made everything, the sun, the moon, the stars, the seas, the animals, night and day, the fish, everything. When he had it all finished, he made man. He put him in a perfect world, like a great, beautiful park. It is called, "The Garden of Eden." He told Adam and Eve they could have everything that was in it but one thing. He wanted them to know that he was above all, so he tested them to see if they would be disobedient. They disobeyed. In so doing they pulled the shade down on this window throwing the whole world into darkness. Their children and their children's children were exactly like them, born to disobey, and from that day to this, all have been born with disobedient hearts and will, and this includes all of us. When the shade of this window was pulled down, God put in another window.

THE LIGHT OF THE LAW

Moses was chosen by God and God took him up on Mt. Sinai. There he gave him the Ten Commandments. But the people defied the law of the Ten Commandments. As Moses came down from the Mount, the people were worshipping a golden calf made from the trinkets of the camp. (Ex. 32:1-8). In doing this they were breaking the very first law of the ten commandments. This law said, "Thou shalt have no other gods before me" (Ex. 20:3). So the people pulled down the shade. The world became darker and darker because the people got farther and farther away from God, and the law was faced with failure.

THE LIGHT OF THE JUDGES

"And the children of Israel did evil in the sight of the Lord" (Judges 2:11).

Now God set judges over them to help control the land, but over and over again the people walked in their evil ways. (Judges 2:19, 3:7, 3:12, 4:1, 6:1, 9:6, 13:1). Because they rejected the light from this window, it too had its shade drawn to keep out the light.

THE LIGHT OF THE KINGS

Having been ineffective with the lights of the Garden, the Law and the Judges, God now provided Kings to rule. (Judges 17:6) - "In those days there was no king in Israel but every man did that which was right in his own eyes."

Some of the kings were good and some were bad, but the people's hearts continued to be rebellious and disobedient, so the shade was pulled down on this window too.

THE LIGHT OF THE PROPHETS

Now God set up a line of prophets who were especially

called by him. They were like fiery preachers and they warned the people to return to the Lord or there would be an unwelcome payday of judgment.

Jesus gave a summary of the treatment the people gave the prophets when he said,"O Jerusalem, Jerusalem, which killest the prophets, and stonest them that are sent unto thee: how often would I have gathered thy children together, as a hen doth gather her brood under her wings, and ye would not!" (Luke 13:34).

THE LIGHT OF GOD'S LOVE

After the shades of the five windows had been pulled down to keep out the light that God was trying to give, there was now only one window left. (Review the five previous windows)

The window of the Garden
The window of the Law
The window of the Judges
The window of the Kings
The window of the Prophets

GOD'S FINAL PLAN

(Point to each window as you recall them).

Now God made one more desperate effort to reveal his full plan. It was a PLAN OF LOVE. He sent his Son, the Lord Jesus as the only light that was left. Some of you may say, "Well, how will he show his love?" He already has. (Fold Fig. 6 to Fig. 9 and cut on line XY and show the cross). God has already proved the light of his love, for God so loved that he gave his Son. He was born in Bethlehem,lived in Galilee,died on Calvary was raised from the dead at Jerusalem and went back to heaven from Mt. Olivet, and soon will be coming back for his own people choosing only those who are his.

TAKE IT OR LEAVE IT

Jesus said, "I am the door." He is the only door, the final door. That door is wide open now. Whosoever will may enter. Jesus stands on the other side of the door, whispering to you, "Come in my child. If any man enter he shall be saved."

One door and only one,
And yet its sides are two,
I'm on the inside,
On which side are you?

CHAPTER 4

LITTLE IS MUCH WHEN GOD IS IN IT

Give and it shall be given unto you; good measure, pressed down and shaken together and running over, shall men give unto your bosom. For with the same measure that ye mete, withal, it shall be measured to you again. (Luke 6:38)

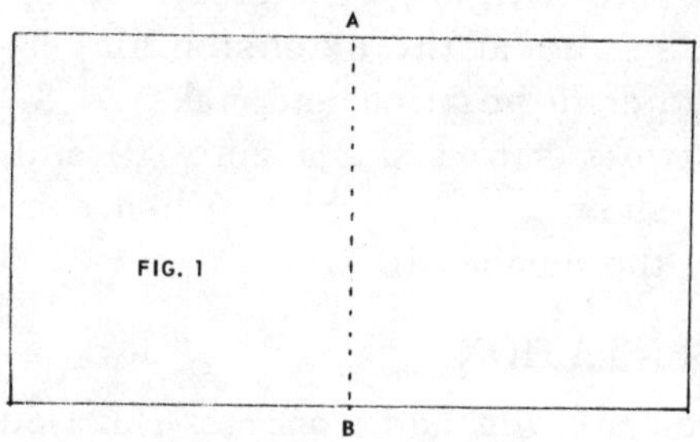

FIG. 1

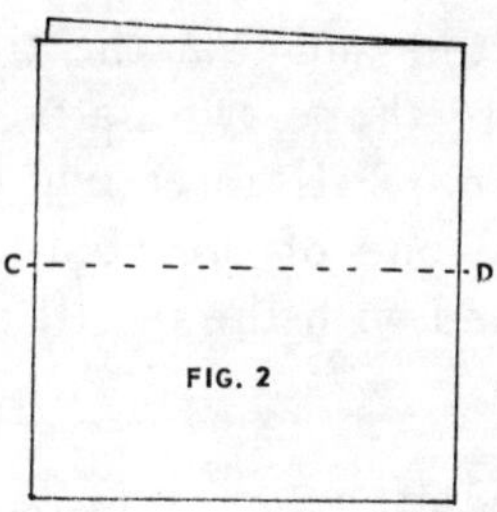

FIG. 2

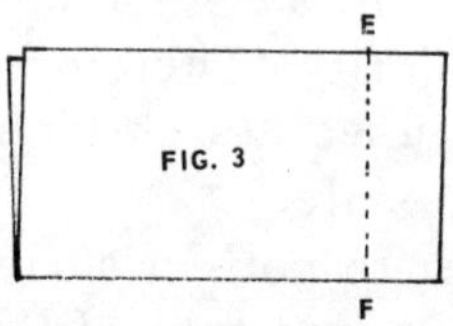

FIG. 3

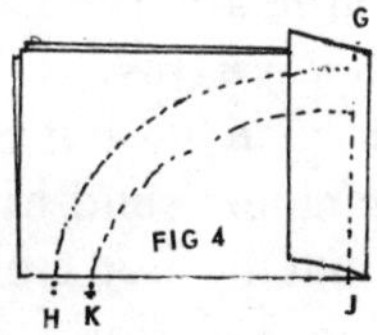

FIG 4

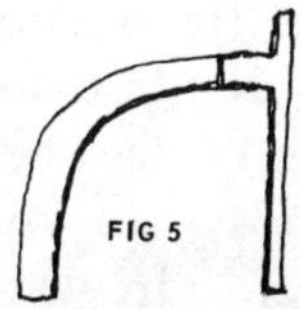
FIG 5

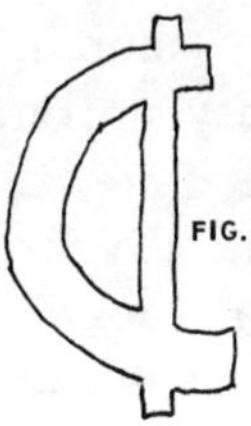
FIG. 6

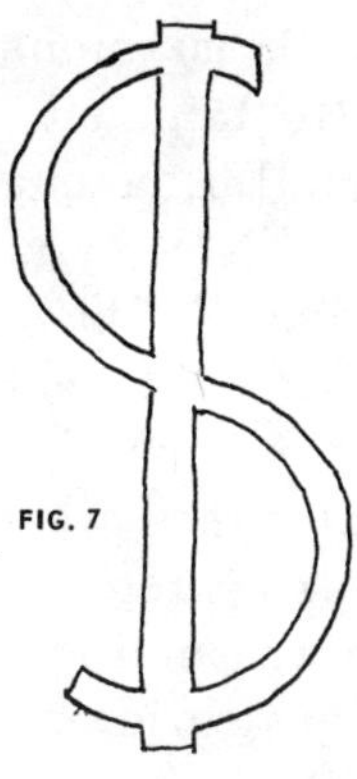
FIG. 7

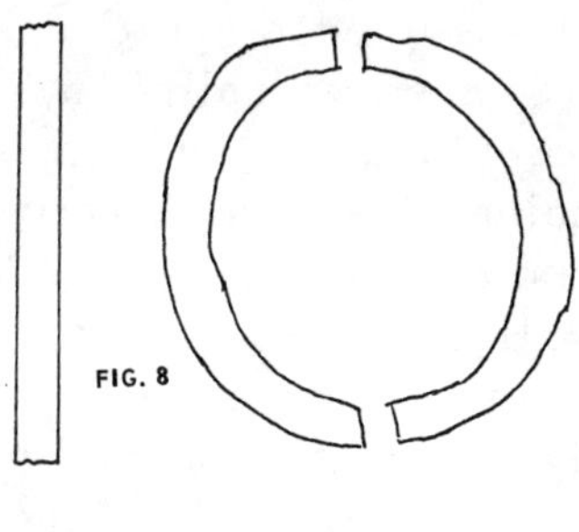
FIG. 8

PROPERTY

A piece of construction paper 5 X 8 inches in size and scissors.

PREPARATION

Prefold Fig. 1 on line AB and Fig. 2 on line CD and Fig. 3 on line EF. Pencil mark lines GH and JK on Fig. 4. Unfold and you are ready for the lesson.

PROCEDURE

During the lesson, fold object to Fig. 4 and cut on lines GH and JK. It will look like Fig 5. Unfold to all but the last fold and it will look like a figure ¢ (Fig. 6). Later, unfold and tear the two ¢'s apart at the extension hinges. Hold these two parts together in position and make a $ sign. Still later cut the two ¢'s to make a zero (0) and use one of the posts and show as a 1, which, when combined with the 0 will make the number 10.

PRESENTATION

Well, boys and girls, you are you and I am me. But God is more. He is One in Three for He is the Father, Son and Holy Spirit, so he is always in the majority. Therefore, little is much when God is in it, but God uses his children to multiply his work, his money and his people.

A little girl was sent out by her mother to collect money for missions. She came to a miser's home and told of the need. He didn't believe in God, missions or the church, but he liked the little girl. He laid out a twenty dollar bill, a silver dollar, a half dollar, a quarter, a dime, a nickel and a penny. He said, "Now, you can have your choice. Take whichever you want." The little girl looked them over and said, "Mother always taught me to take the smallest piece, so I will take this one." She reached for the dime. Then she said, "Mister this piece is so small, I might lose it. You wont mind if I wrap it up in that piece of paper, will you?" Then she wrapped it up in the twenty dollar bill. Yes, God does use his children to multiply his work, his money and his people.

THE MIRACLE OF MULTIPLICATION

God has great arithmetic. He takes one little apple seed and from it comes many bushels of apples, through his soil, sunshine, showers and seasons. A small boy's lunch fed 5000 hungry people (Mark 14:17-21). If God can multiply bushels of barley from single seeds, it would be no problem for him to multiply whole barley loaves from a hungry lad's lunch basket.

If God can multiply thousands of fish from a thimble full of fish eggs, he can produce enough fish to feed the multitude from the sacrificial offering of a boy who was more excited by 5000 people than he was by two dead fish.

The jaw-bone of an ass slew 1000 men when the Spirit of God came upon the super-man, Samson(Judges 15:15). Little is much when God is in it.

DOUBLE DIVIDENDS

Now let's talk about what everybody wants most and has little of - Money. (Fold Fig. 1 to Fig. 4 and cut lines GH and JK and show the ¢.

A moment ago I had no cents(sense), but now I have one. I hope it will multiply like the loaves and fishes. If you have some cents like this in your purse and another kind in your head, and Jesus in your heart, you might some day become a millionaire. Hey, look, I have already doubled it (Tear the two apart at the extension hinge).

NO CREDIT CARDS, PLEASE

Now, if I could make a dollar out of these two cents, I wonder how much of it would belong to God? (Hold the two parts together to form a $ sign). How much is Gods? Not five cents or fifty cents, but all of it. God is so good.. He doesn't say you are to give him the whole dollar, but he does say you are to give him a tenth, which he calls the tithe. This is just a token by which you say that all belongs to him. After you have set aside a dime out of the dollar, you can give as much more as you can and as he has prospered you.

THE BARGAIN BASEMENT

I want two children to come and help me. They will be God's Bankers. Pleased to meet you Mr. Rockefeller and John D. Junior. I will share this dollar with you. (Cut to Fig. 8) Here is one for you and here is nothing for you. 1 and 0 make 10. There, that is God's dime from the dollar. You had two cents, but God made a dollar out of it. Now you say, "Thank you" by giving him a tenth and keeping 90 cents. Yes, that is a great bargain, because little is much when God is in it.

AN UNPUBLISHED LAW OF LOVE

Little is said about the tithe in the New Testament. That is because as far back as Abraham all the people honored God with their tithe of grain, fruit, flocks and money. It was such an old law and was so well practiced that it was needless to even mention it in the New Testament. It would be like saying, "Open your mouth when you take a bite" or "put your feet on the ground when you walk" or "make a noise when you holler."

THE TITHE THAT GOT TOO BIG

A little boy began to tithe. It wasn't very much for he seldom got a dollar, but when he did, he gave God a dime. When he reached high School he cut lawns in the summer time and shoveled snow in the winter, for pay. Then he began to cheat God, keeping for himself a portion of God's tithe. When he finished college he made a big salary and his tithe was much larger than it had been. But he continued to cheat God, or to rob him as Malachi said in Malachi 3:8.

THE CHEAT WHO CHANGED HIS MIND

Finally this young man went to his pastor and explained that when he was a little fellow he could give a dime from his dollars but now it was hard to part with a tenth of his big salary each week. The wise pastor said,"Well we can remedy that. Let's pray about it." Eagerly the young man got on his knees at the side of the pastor. Then he heard the pastor pray, "Dear Lord, you have blest this young man with a big salary, and now his tithe is so big, he finds it hard to give so much. Please, dear Lord, bring his salary down so he wont have to give so much to your work. Reduce his pay, dear Lord, real quick so he can begin to give less right away."

The young man interrupted the pastor's prayer, and cried, "No, no, dear Lord, don't answer that prayer. Thank you Lord for being so generous with my wages. Please don't let me receive less so I can give less, but let me receive more so I can give more. Thank you, Lord, thank you, Lord."

Boys and girls, if you want dollars, be honest before God with your cents, for little is much when God is in it. Here is a verse to live by - "Give and it shall be given unto you; good measure, pressed down and shaken together and running over, shall men give unto your bosom. For with the same measure that ye mete, withal, it shall be measured to you again." (Luke 6:38).

CHAPTER 5

BIBLE BALLS AND CHAINS

Foolishness is bound in the heart of a child; but the rod of correction shall drive it far from him.

(Proverbs 22:15)

PROPERTY

A sheet of newsprint or other thin paper, 20 X 20 inches in size, pencil and scissors.

PREPARATION

Prefold Fig. 1 on line AB and Fig. 2 on line CD and Fig. 3 on line EF and Fig. 4 on line GH. Mark lightly with pencil, line JK and LM of Fig. 5. Unfold and you are ready for the lesson.

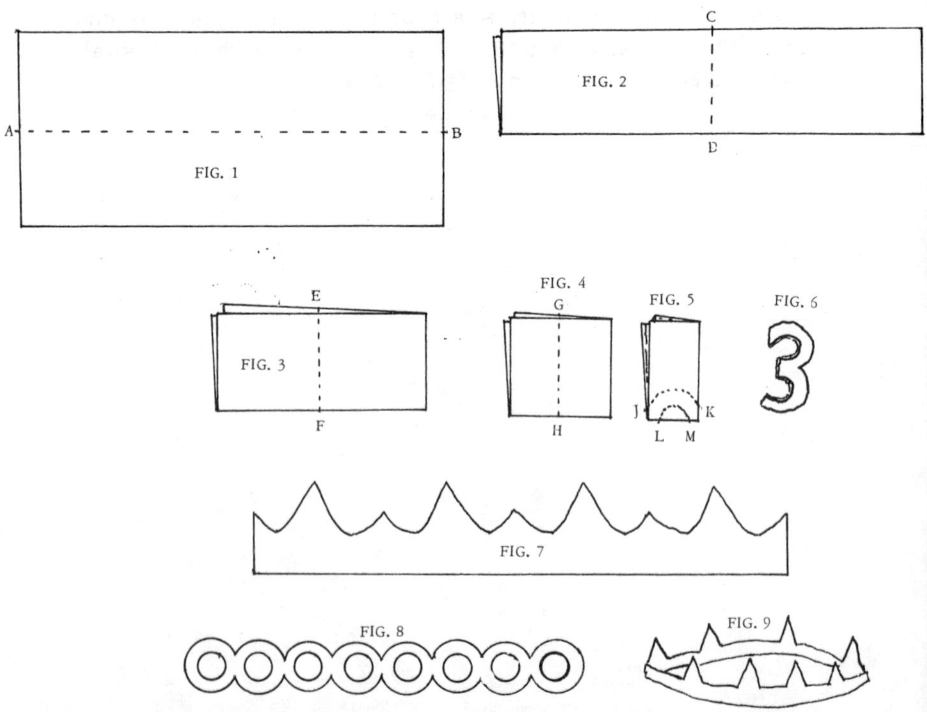

PROCEDURE

During the lesson, fold to Fig. 5 and cut on lines JK and LM, cutting so the hinges are not destroyed. The curved section when partly unfolded will become the number 3 (Fig. 6) and a chain (Fig. 8) when completely unfolded. There will be two identical upper sections, one to represent a prison wall and the other to be like a crown when the two ends are held together (Figs. 7 and 9).

PRESENTATION

How many of you have ever done any downright foolish things, like gritting your teeth when you are angry or stomping your feet when you can't have your own way or sticking your tongue out at your mother when she scolds you? And listen, when you sass your mother or say mean things, you are letting the love God put in your heart escape through a little trap door, your mouth.

Well, Proverbs 22:15 says that foolishness is bound in the heart of a child, but the rod of correction shall drive it far from him.

Remember, that paddle in your mother's hand is in the hand of one who loves you and every time the clap of that paddle sends out its echo from your tail section, it hurts her more than it does you. She is trying to raise you right by starting at the bottom - your bottom. She ties up the dog at night, so why should you run loose?

NOT ANGER BUT LOVE

God doesn't have a paddle, but he has other ways to correct you. However, it is never out of anger but always out of love, for "whom the Lord loveth he chasteneth" (Heb. 12:6).

THE HAPPINESS KIT

Did you ever feel that your parents or your teachers were too strict, and you wished you could do as you pleased? So did I. As a child, I was just like you because such foolishness also bound my childish heart. When I talked back to my mother, she not only listened to my word, but also to my heartbeat. Now that I am grown, I am grateful to my parents for their loving guidance by their slap stick measures of correction for it drove the foolishness from my heart. Once it was just a one way love from them to me but now it is two way. I love them because they first loved me. Family happiness is not made in heaven. It comes in a do-it-yourself kit. You have to put it together yourself.

THREE BIBLE CHAINS

I am going to cut out a chain because that is what this lesson is all about. I will talk about three chains.

THE CHAIN OF CREATION
THE CHAIN OF CORRECTION
THE CHAIN OF CONCERN.

(Fold Fig. 1 to Fig. 5 and cut on lines JK and LM. Keep all the sections except the small round bottom pieces.

THE CHAIN OF CREATION

(Unfold the first two half loops of the chain section and show the number 3). The Chain of Creation could also be called the Chain of Command which is a soldier's jargon. It means the passing down of orders from a higher authority to a lower, like an order from a Colonel to a Major to a Captain to a Lieutenant to a sergeant to a Private. It would be like a suggestion from your teacher to your mother who passes it on to your father who in turn then passes it on to you to be obeyed.

THE THREE-FOLD CHAIN OF COMMAND

God had a chain of command in the Creation. There are three. (Hold up 3). There was the Father, the Son and the Holy Spirit. For instance, in the book of Genesis, these three consulted together about the Creation. God said, "Let US make man in OUR image after OUR likeness" (Gen. 1:26).

When Adam and Eve disobeyed an order, God had to correct them. "And the Lord God said, Behold the man is become one of US" (Gen. 3:22) Later, after sin began to show its ugly head when the tower of Babel was being built on the plains of Shinar so its peak would reach heaven, God said, "Let US go there and confound their language" (Gen. 11:7).

Their foolishness was dealt with through the threefold Chain of Command and Correction by the Father, the Son and the Holy Spriit, the Three In One.

GOD TRIED

After man had sinned so long and God's laws were broken so wilfully, God decided to try love. He sent Jesus. (John 3:18). But the son was rejected (John 1:12) and was nailed to a cross. Then God sent another Comforter, the Holy Spirit (John 14:16). He is here now making God's final effort with foolish, wayward hearts, like mine and yours. That lump in your throat when you are alone, that sorrow that comes after any departure from God's law, is put there by the Holy Spirit. He comes not only to comfort but to reprove you of sin and righteousness and judgment (John 16:8).

THE CHAIN OF CORRECTION

(Unfold the complete chain of eight links).

I have often seen prisoners working on the roads. Their ankles had chains on them. They were guarded with guns in daytime and at night they were locked up in cells, behind walls that looked like this (Show Fig. 7) with high towers occupied by guards with guns to keep the prisoners from escaping. These are the Chains of Correction for crimes committed.

THE GOOD NEWS

You may not know it, but you too have a chain around your young hearts, a chain of bad habits. You were born with a nature that makes you that way. You have chosen to go the wrong way and now the devil has shackled you by these habits. But I have good news for you. "If the Son shall make you free, you shall be free indeed (John 8:36).

THE CHAIN OF CONCERN

Some of you say, "Teacher, I want to be free. I have bad habits. I am a slave, bound by Satan's chains. He has handcuffs on me!" (Tear off two of the circles and show what handcuffs look like).

I am glad you know it, my child. Your Sunday School teachers knows it, your father and mother know it. All are praying for you that you might be delivered from these shackles of self will. They have organized a secret prayer chain and have joined hands and hearts with others, asking God for your deliverance. They believe what the Bible says about it in Matthew 18:19 - "That if two of you shall agree on earth as touching anything that they shall ask, it shall be done for them of my Father which is in heaven, for where two or three are gathered together in my Name, there am I in the midst of them."

BE A HAPPY SLAVE WITH THE RIGHT MASTER

(Hold up the prison wall again). This is a wall of concrete. You can trade it today for a crown of Gold. Look. (Quickly hold ends together showing Fig. 9). You have a choice today. What will it be? A concrete wall with the Master Devil as your prison warden or the golden crown with the Savior as your shepherd, leading you to the green pastures and beside the still water? Bear the cross here that you may wear the crown hereafter. If you MUST be bound by a chain, let it be as the slave of Jesus with an honorable CHAIN.

CHAPTER 6

BEGINNING AT THE BEGINNING

"And now also the axe is laid unto the root of the tree; therefore every tree that bringeth not forth good fruit is hewn down and cast into the fire." (Matth. 3:10)

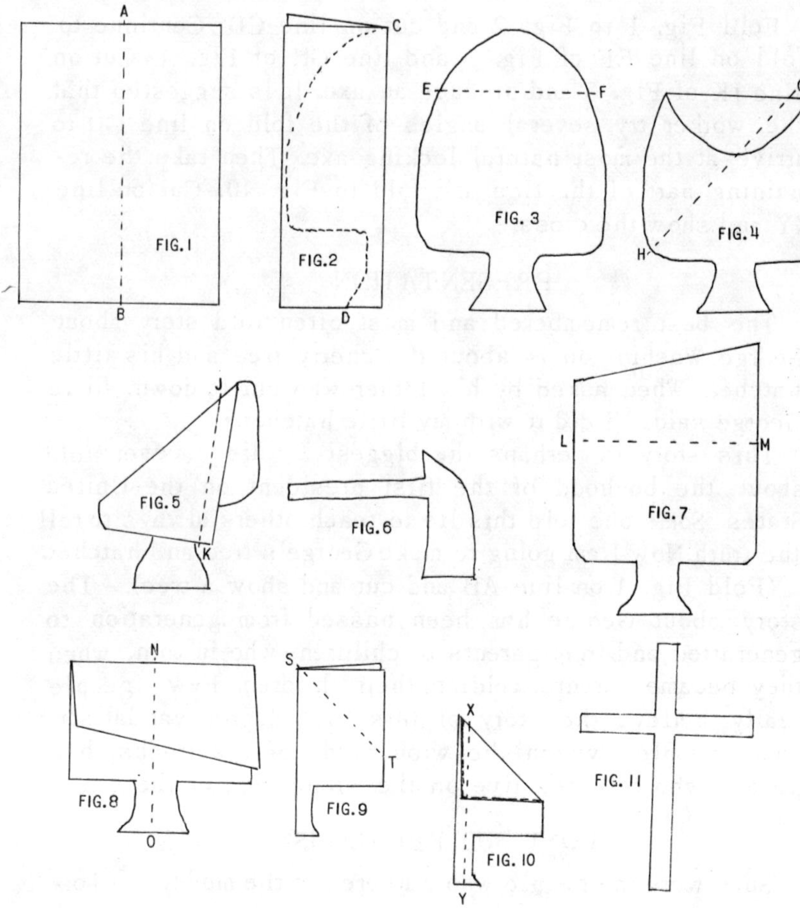

PROPERTY

A sheet of paper 5X12 inches in size and scissors.

PREPARATION

Fold Fig. 1 on line AB. Pencil mark a half tree as on CD of Fig. 2. Fold Fig. 3 on line EF and again on line GH of Fig. 4. Pencil lightly line JK on Fig. 5. Unfold and it is ready to use in the lesson.

PROCEDURE

Fold Fig. 1 to Fig. 2 and cut on line CD. Continue to fold on line EF of Fig. 3 and line GH of Fig. 4. Cut on line JK of Fig. 5 and produce an axe. It is suggested that the worker try several angles of the fold on line GH to arrive at the most natural looking axe. Then take the remaining part of the tree and fold to Fig. 10. Cut on line XY and show the cross.

PRESENTATION

The best remembered and most often told story about George Washington is about the cherry tree and his little hatchet. When asked by his father who cut it down, little George said, "I did it with my little hatchet."

This story is perhaps the biggest lie ever told about the boyhood of the first president on the United States. Some one told this lie to teach others always to tell the truth. Now I am going to make George's tree and hatchet.

(Fold Fig. 1 on line AB and cut and show a tree). The story about George has been passed from generation to generation and from parents to children, who in turn, when they became parents, told it to their children. Few people really believe the story of this first degree vandalism. Some people live on the wrong side of the tracks, but people who tell lies live on the wrong side of the truth.

LOST BUT RELIGIOUS

Such were the people who gathered at the muddy Jordan River, and who stood in line, waiting to be baptized by John the Baptist. They came in great numbers, beggars, merchant-men, tax gatherers, fishermen, the self employed, the riff raff, the scribes and the Pharisees, the women, the children, entire families. They were adventure seekers and excitement hungry hypocrites. Many could not say why they were there, except that they just happened along and joined the crowd and fell in line. They did not realize that if they were baptized in their careless insincerity, they would go into the river dry sinners and come out wet ones, but still sinners, unless they first showed deep sorrow for their sins and then forsake them.

THE ROUGH SHOD PREACHER

John The Baptist, the faithful, rough shod, plain talking preacher lowered the boom on them for their insincerity. Looking over the line-up he cried, "O you generation of vipers, who hath warned you to flee from the wrath to come? Bring forth fruits meet for repentance. The axe is laid already unto the root of the trees." (Matth. 3:8,10). (Fold Fig. 4 and cut on line JK and show axe).

HIGH-TONED HYPOCRITES

These insincere, hypocritical religionists were like an ornamental radio that would not play and like a car with silk upholstery and a gold steering wheel that would not run and like a newly painted red pump on a dry well. To a group of true followers of the Lord Jesus, they would have looked like a cukoo in a chicken coup, who would sit contentedly on a nest but never lay an egg. Jesus said in Matth. 7:18-20 - "A corrupt tree bringeth forth evil fruit. Every tree that bringeth not forth good fruit is cut down and cast into the fire. Wherefore by their fruits shall ye know them."

WARNING THE UNWARY

John the Baptist saw the trademark of sin and unbelief in the hearts of most of these people and he warned them not to play with sacred things. Jesus said, "Not everyone that saith Lord, Lord, shall enter into the kingdom of heaven" (Matth. 7:21).

WHAT A CHRISTIAN IS LIKE

Christians are pictured as trees. There are many kinds of trees, like the oak tree, the pine tree, the willow tree, the maple tree, the sycamore tree, the linden tree, the aspen tree and the giant redwood tree. But the Christian is to be like a fruit tree, like the apple, peach, cherry or pear tree. Jesus was saying that as the fruit of the apple tree is apples, so the fruit of the Christian is Christian fruits, like being sorry for your sins, so sorry that you will give them up and never again to return to them. That is what John The Baptist meant when he said, "Repent."

Jesus described people, such as John saw at Jordan, as graves with beautiful white gravestones but inwardly full of dead men's bones (Matth. 23). John warned the noisy crowd at Jordan not to be fruitless trees, subject to the woodsman's axe. He preached that the first fruit is repentance. He said, "The axe is laid already to the root of the tree."

FIRST THINGS FIRST

I hope you will use the axe on your sins before God must use it on the roots of the tree of your young lives. You may feel unable to 'go it alone' but you can blaze a trail, no matter how dull your axe may be. Don't come through the waters of Jordan unless you have first come through the cleansing fountain of the blood of Christ.

We used to sing

Some through the water,
Some through the flood,
Some through great trial,
But ALL through the blood.

MAKING SURE OF THE FIRST STEP

Do not profess the Savior unless you first possess him, or you will be like one of the Roman soldiers at the cross. When they gambled for the cloak that Jesus wore, he won it. He put on the garment, wearing Jesus on the outside but not having him on the inside.

Paul later wrote in Romans 6:4 . "Therefore we are buried with him by baptism into death, that like as Christ was raised . . . so we should walk in newness of life."

A CHRISTIAN'S PROUD PORTRAYAL

A Christian is the only picture unsaved people ever see of Jesus. You are where he lives, you are his house here on earth. You are the picture of Jesus on display. Show him up with the richest colors, set in the finest frame and under the brightest lights. Let them see HIM through YOU. Instead of God coming to your fruitless tree with an axe, why not come to his tree, the cross, in simple childlike faith, which is full of the fruits of salvation. (Fold Fig. 7 to Fig. 10 and cut on line XY and show the cross).

CHAPTER 7

ACROBATIC CHRISTIANS

Then we which are alive and remain shall be caught up together with them in the clouds to meet the Lord in the air and so shall we ever be with the Lord.

(1 Thess.4: 17).

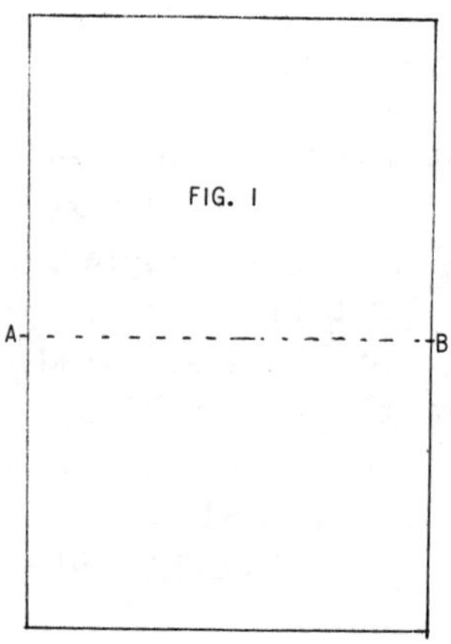

FIG. 1

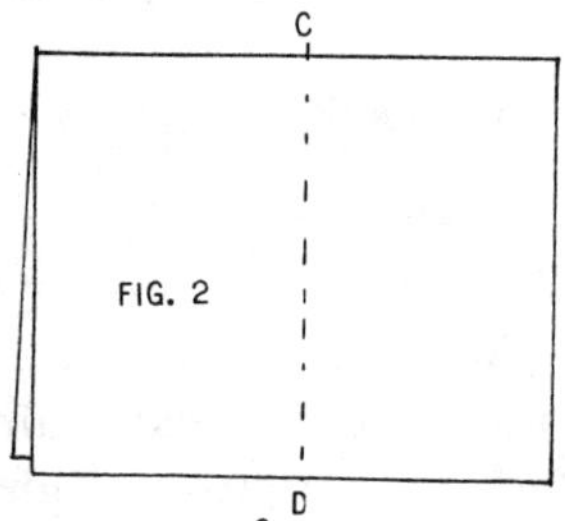

FIG. 2

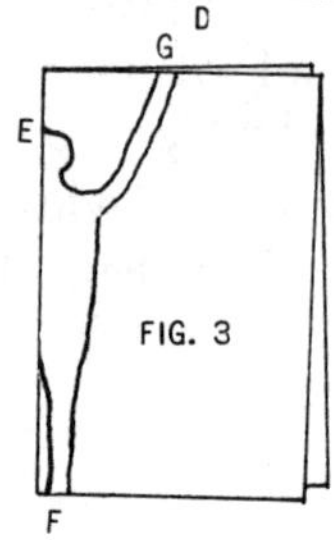

FIG. 3

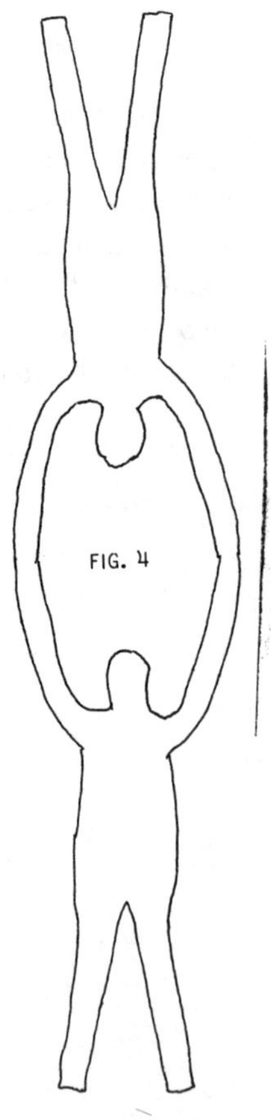

FIG. 4

PROPERTY

A sheet of paper 5 X 12 inches in size, and scissors.

PREPARATION

Fold Fig. 1 on line AB and Fig. 2 on line CD. Lightly pencil mark as best you can, the half body of an acrobat with his arms extended to the upper hinge, letting the arm lines run off the paper to retain the hinge when cutting line EFG of Fig. 3. Unfold to be ready for the lesson demonstration.

PROCEDURE

Fold Fig. 1 on line AB and Fig. 2 on line CD. Cut on pencil lines EFG of Fig. 3 so when unfolded you will have two high wire acrobats meeting in the air, with hands locked.

PRESENTATION

Nearly everyone was been to a circus or carnival or County Fair and has seen tight rope walkers and acrobats on flying trapezes. If you have not seen this in a tent or building, you perhaps have seen it on television.

Usually there are two high platforms, one on each end of the building or tent and there are dangling ropes that are fastened above. They look like swings.

THE FLYING ACROBATS

At a given signal one acrobat swings out into the air toward the center of the arena clinging to the bar at the end of the rope and at exactly the right split second, the other leaves his perch and also swings out. In mid-air the first one is caught by the second at the ankles. Then again, at the exact second, as both are swinging, the unoccupied bar returns. The one acrobat releases the other from his firm hold and in mid-air, he catches the moving bar and it returns him safely to his perch. The two acrobats may change their routine with flub dubs in mid-air but no matter what their procedure, one must always catch the other. While they are performing, they look something like this. (Fold Fig. 1 to Fig. 3 and cut carefully on pencil lines).

CHRISTIANS GO BY ACROBATIC RULES

Acrobats are not all Christians, but Christians are like acrobats if they truly live for the Lord. There are five things that acrobats do that remind me of how Christians should do.

PILGRIMS SEEKING A BETTER COUNTRY

1. AN ACROBAT PERFORMS FROM A HIGH PLATEAU.

Christians must live temporarily on the low levels of earth but they must perform according to the high levels of heaven. They are IN the world but are not OF the world. They are pilgrims in a strange land and are like the patriarchs of Heb. 11, Abraham, Isaac, Jacob, Enoch, Sara, Moses, Gideon, Barak, David, Samuel and others. They seek a better country, that is an heavenly (Heb. 11:16).

LOOKING UNTO JESUS

Christians must keep their eyes heavenward for that is where their high plateau is, looking unto Jesus the author and finisher of their faith, laying aside every weight and the sin that doth so easily beset them (Heb. 12:1).

FULL SURRENDER

2. THE ACROBAT MUST HAVE FAITH IN ANOTHER.

An acrobat, when he leaves his swing in high mid-air must have absolute faith in another acrobat who is to grasp him to keep him from plunging, headlong to his death on the sawdust floor below. He must have faith to believe that the other acrobat has strength to hold him until he catches his swinging bar that he might be safely swung back to his platform.

PAUL SERENE WITH A CREPE ON HIS DOOR

A Christian must have this kind of faith in the One God

has provided, his only Son, the Lord Jesus. The Apostle Paul had this kind of faith in another as he sat in solitary in the prison in Rome. He had given up hope for this life for he knew he was to be killed by having his head cut off but he wrote to his young friend and fellow worker, Timothy, saying, "I know whom I have believed and am persuaded that he is able to keep that which I have committed unto him against that day." (2 Timothy 1:12).

PERSONAL FAITH

I had that kind of faith when I was brought out of the depths of my sin. I came to believe Isaiah 53:6 - "All we like sheep have gone astray; we have turned everyone to his own way, but the Lord hath laid on him the iniquity of us all".

TRUSTING ANOTHER FOR LIFE

3. THE ACROBAT MUST LET GO.

The acrobat cannot complete his thrilling performance unless he is willing to let go and put himself in the hands of another.

The same performance in the Christian's life can only be completed if there is a willingness to let go and let God. Everything must be entrusted to him who is able to keep you from falling and to present you faultless before the presence of his glory, with exceeding joy. (Jude 24).

The Apostle Paul is most urgent about this when he says, "I beseech you brethren by the mercies of God that you present your bodies a living sacrifice . . . which is your reasonable service" (Rom. 12:1).

RIGHT TIMING

4. THE ACROBAT MUST REACH OUT.

The acrobat must do his part if he is to be saved from certain death, and he must do it in time. He reaches out but not too late, thus giving the other acrobat his stretched out arms so they can be firmly grabbed.

THE STOREHOUSE OF GOD

The child of God must also reach out, and on time, to take what God has already given him. He reaches out by faith for salvation, and through prayer receives all the goodies offered from the storehouse of God.

If you sat at a table that was loaded with food and you went away hungry, you just didn't reach out or you didn't ask for food to be passed. If you fail to reach out, you have not because you ask not (James 4:2).

THE WEDDING IN THE SKIES

5. THE ACROBAT MEETS HIS RESCUER IN THE AIR.

A rescuer or savior is one who saves. If you are a child of God, you too are to meet your Savior in the air when he comes for all those who belong to his family. This great event is called the RAPTURE of the church or the catching up of all believers. Jesus will come down and you will go up. (Show object again, fully opened with arms of acrobats joined in a clasp).

NOW IS THE TIME

This meeting in the air is mentioned in 1 Thess. 4:17 - "Then we which are alive . . . shall be caught up together to meet the Lord in the air, and so shall we ever be with the Lord".

Just as the acrobat must be ready to be met by the one who will save him, so you must be ready to meet the coming one. His coming will be like a thief in the night, unannounced. In the meantime, be watching and waiting, for "Ye know neither the day nor the hour wherein the son of man cometh" (Matth. 25:13).

CHAPTER 8

BIRTHDAY SHOES

If we walk in the light as he is in the light, we have fellowship one with another and the blood of Jesus Christ, His Son, cleanseth us from all sin

(1 John 1:7).

PROPERTY

A sheet of paper 9 X 9 inches square and scissors.

PREPARATION

Prefold Fig. 1 on line AB. Pencil lightly the profile of a half heart. Prefold Fig. 4 on line GH to Fig. 5 and mark lightly with a pencil, line JK. Unfold for lesson.

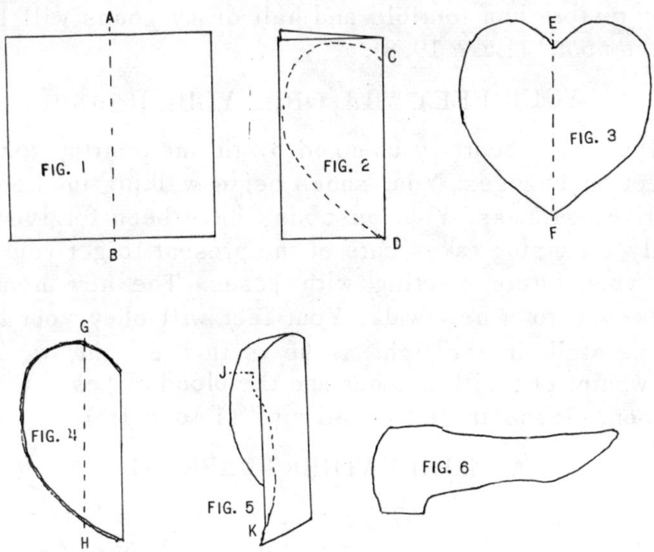

PROCEDURE

Fold to Fig. 2 and cut out the half heart. Fold to Fig. 5 and cut on line JK. The result will be a pair of shoes.

PRESENTATION

Could anyone be born with his heart in his shoes? This is not possible in your first birth which is the birth of your body. But Jesus spoke about a second birth or new birth. This is a spiritual birth (John 3:3).

Such a spiritual birth would not be healthy or normal if it did not affect your shoes and your walk, and the hands, the eyes, the mouth, the ears and every other part of your body. When you are born again, everything becomes new. (2 Cor. 5:17). Certainly, when you have this new birth your walk as a Christian will lead on new and better paths. It made a tremendous change in the life style of Paul and Zaccheus. Saul stopped throwing Christians into jail, and Zaccheus said, "If I have taken anything from any man, I will restore him fourfold and half of my goods will I give to the poor" (Luke 19:8).

YOUR FEET WILL OBEY YOUR HEART

When your heart is changed by the new birth, your life direction changes. Your shoes begin walking in the paths of righteousness. Your past sins have been forgiven and daily cleansing takes care of the present to get you ready for your future meeting with Jesus. The new heart directs you to a new walk. Your feet will obey your heart. "If we walk in the light as he is in the light, we have fellowship, one with another and the blood of Jesus Christ, His Son, cleanseth us from all sin" (1 John 1:7).

A GRANDFATHERS WARNING

Methusaleh lived 969 years but that was before automobiles and cocktail bars and taverns. Those snake pits turn drinking drivers loose to sit behind steering wheels. They are incapable of steering so they just aim. They have unsteady vision. They see what is not there and hit what is there. It has been said that true Christians drink GIN; that is H_2O, Hydrogen and Oxygen, which is water. Some call water 'Adam's Ale'.

An old drunken grandfather warned his grandsons about the CATCHUP bottle. He said, "Boys when you come to a saloon (cocktail bar, tavern) always run past it or the devil will pull you in as he did me." He called it the CATCHUP bottle because it CATCHES UP with so many.

The true Christian has become more than a conqueror over what an ancient poet called

A bar to heaven, a door to hell,
Whoever named it, named it well.

A true child of God gets a new heart and shoes to match. These shoes will run past the places where the devil's brew is poured into the bloodstream. (Cut out heart from Fig. 2).

A 2,000 MILE WALK

Suppose you set out to walk from Chicago to Los Angeles. You would begin that long trek by taking a single step in the direction of the seaside city. Then you would walk, walk, walk. You would cross the Mississippi River, the Missouri River, The Colorado River, the Rocky Mountains, the Cascades and the Mojave Desert. You would wear out several pairs of shoes so I am going to cut cut a pair of shoes for you. (Fold Fig. 3 to Fig. 5 and cut on line JK and show shoes).

STRENGTH FOR THE DAY

Each day you walked you would receive strength for the day, just as you do in the Christian walk. The walk to California and the Christian walk are not easy, but certainly possible. Every night after your long walk you might feel you need a couple of leg transplants.

What about sore feet? The soreness might not be from the long walk or the height of the mountain passes, but from the little pebble in your shoe, or unless your shoes were too small. Hugh Downs once said, "Size 9 is my size, but size 10 feels so good I always buy size 11."

HARDSHIPS BEFORE HEAVEN

As a Christian, you must be prepared for hardship. The Israelites got to the promised land only after they crossed the wilderness with its fiery serpents and dry, thirsty land and the monotonous manna as Angel food from heaven, plus a daily allotment of quail, without French fries or potato chips or Pepsi.

In your walk with the Lord there will be timesofself denial and it will seem that your life will have a hopeless end, but one day it will turn out to be an endless hope. "Be thou faithful unto death and I will give thee a crown of life" (Rev. 2:10)

MOTHER'S GOO TURNED TO YUM YUM

A chocolate cake is not appetizing when Mother takes some dry flour and then slops in some thick distasteful sour milk and on top of that throws in some raw eggs and whips it all into a sticky 'goo'. When you think of it you say "Yuk." When this pan of goo is put into the oven, the different ingredients fall in love with each other and begin to hug one another and it turns out to become one sweet family. When the icing is tenderly troweled on you beginto dribble. When Mother serves you, the slices are too thin and Mother is so stingy for a cake that is so good. You ask for seconds and daringly for thirds. Now, instead of "Yuk" it's "Yum, Yum."

Your walk through the Christian life will have some sour milk and dry flour, but the end will be an iced cake.

REACHING FOR THE HIGHER PLATEAUS

A six year old boy had some talent for drawing, but he never finished the top of his pictures. When asked, "Why" he said, "I can't reach the top." There is yet much to be reached, but it can only be reached if you walk in heavenly shoes with your new heart in them. The short biography of Enoch was written in twelve words, "Enoch walked with God, and he was not, for God took him." (Gen. 5:24). There is a great, exciting journey ahead for each of you. You do not make it by car or plane. You walk it. If you are a true child of God, you must act, talk, live and walk like one, walking worthy of the calling wherewith you have been called. (Eph. 4:1).

THE STEADY WALK

Isaiah told the people about "the bread of adversity." He said, "This is the way, walk ye in it."(Is. 30:21). To the church at Rome, the Apostle Paul said, "Let us walk honestly." (Rom. 13:13). To the church at Corinth he said, "As the Lord hath called . . . so let him walk." (1 Cor. 7:17). The walk with the Lord has no detours and no short cuts.

NO SHORT-CUTS OR DETOURS

A sick patient was ordered by his doctor to walk five miles a day. He obeyed for a few days and then he found short cuts, down alleys and across lots, so finally he was walking only five blocks, but told the doctor he was 'covering' five miles. Though the cemetery was five miles away, he had only a five block ride in the casket coach at his funeral for they took the same short cuts he had been taking, through the alleys and across lots.

There are no heavenly bargain basements. John 14:6 says "I am the way . . .no man cometh unto the Father but by me." How about it, have you gotten your heavenly heart into your earthly shoes, with the toes pointing in the heavenly direction? There are four ways to walk -

Behind him
Ahead of him
Cross-ways to him
With him.
Let there be no either or,
Wisely choose that number four.

CHAPTER 9

THE MISER'S BASKET

''Give and it shall be given unto you, good measure pressed down and shaken together shall men give into your bosom, for with the same measure that ye mete withal it shall be measured to you again.''
(Luke 6:38)

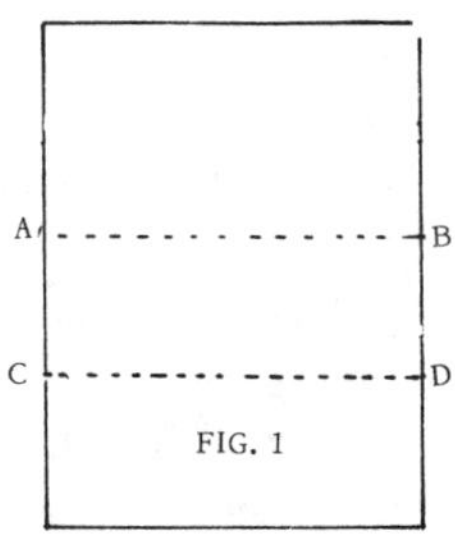

FIG. 1

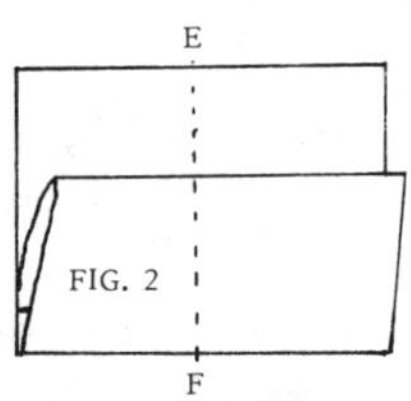

FIG. 2

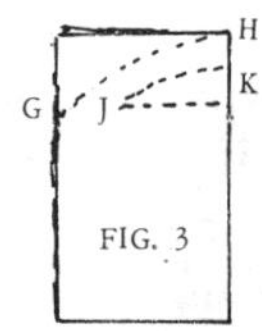

FIG. 3

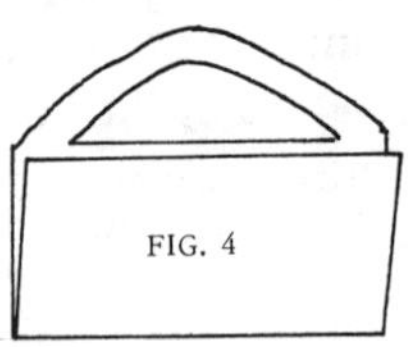
FIG. 4

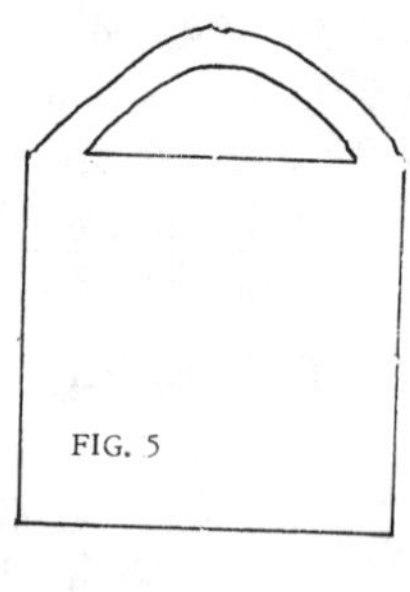
FIG. 5

PROPERTY

A sheet of paper 7 X 11 inches in size and scissors.

PREPARATION

Prefold Fig. 1 on lines AB and CD. Fold Fig. 2 on line EF. Pencil mark lightly lines GH and JK on Fig. 3. Unfold to be ready for the lesson.

PROCEDURE

Fold Fig. 1 to Fig. 3 and cut on lines GH and JK. Unfold to Fig. 4 and show shallow basket. Later, unfold to larger basket (Fig. 5).

PRESENTATION

A mother was trying to teach her young son to help around the house, asking him to do little chores for her, here and there and now and then.

A SELFISH SON

The son had noted that his daddy brought home money each week as pay for the work he had done at the shop. At the end of one week, the mother found a note on the kitchen table, listing all the chores the son had done that week. The list read as follows -

For carryng out the garbige - 10 cents
For goin to the stor 8 cents
For sweepin the bak steps 12 cents
For walkin the dawg 6 cents
For mailin a leter 4 cents
For rakin the leeves 5 cents
For wipin the disshes 5 cents

Totel 50 cents

SIGNED - Tommy

A LOVING MOM

The following night, when he went to bed, he found a shiny new Kennedy half dollar on the bedspread and also a note.He read as follows -

For cooking meals - 0
For making the bed - 0
For mending socks - 0
For doing the laundry - 0
For dusting the furniture - 0
For ironing the clothes - 0
For washing the dishes - 0
For helping with Tommy's homework - 0

Total - 0

SIGNED - Your Loving Mother

It was a lesson Tommy never forgot. He felt like he had thumbed a ride in a wheelbarrow with his mother push- the wheelbarrow.

This mother's love was like a touch of wonder to this lad and it changed an unhappy and selfish son to a son of love. He had used a hammer to gain his end, and his mother had responded with a bouquet of flowers

PUTTING LOVE IN THE RIGHT PLACE

God is like your mother, or perhaps it would be more correct to say your mother is like God. You give so little to her and she gives so much to you.

OSCAR HAMMERSTEIN ONCE WROTE

A bell's not a bell till you ring it,
A song's not a song till you sing it
Love's not put in the heart to stay,
For love's not love till you give it away.

THE BARLEY BISCUIT SANDWICH

One day a small boy gave his lunch basket to Jesus. It had in it five barley biscuits and two fish. It was a lunch prepared by his loving mother. (Cut Fig. 3 on lines GH and JK and show shallow basket - (Fig. 4).

Out of this small basket of lunch, Jesus broke enough bits to feed 5,000 hungry people. (John 6:1-13).

STRANGE ARITHMETIC

Strange arithmetic was used here. The boy SUBTRACTED it from his hungry self and ADDED it to what Jesus could do with it. Jesus DIVIDED it among the people and then MULTIPLIED it so it would feed all those hungry people and still have twelve baskets full left over.

GOD'S UNENDING SUPPLY

With God there is always enough and to spare. He said, "Give and it shall be given unto you, good measure, pressed down and shaken together and running over shall men give into your bosom . . . (Luke 6:38).

God always gives over and above, more exceeding and abundant above what we ask or even think. (Eph.3:18-20). His liberal gifts show up in his willingness to forgive our sins, for he says, "For where sin abounded, grace did MUCH MORE ABOUND" (Rom. 5:20).

THE BIG HANDED, OPEN HEARTED GOD

God's bigger basket shows up all through the Bible. He leads his sheep beside the STILL water (Ps. 23:2) and to the GREEN pastures. When the Prodigal son returned to his father, the father gave him the BEST robe and then killed the FATTED calf.

BEAUTY FOR ASHES

If you need pardon for your sins and your heart is aching over past disobediences, he says, "Let the wicked forsake his way and the unrighteous man his thoughts and let him return unto the Lord, and he will have mercy upon him and will ABUNDANTLY pardon'' (Is. 55:7). Look again at the measly little miserly basket you offer to God and then at the BIG basket he offers you. (Show shallow folded basket again and then drop fold to the larger).

EVERLASTING FRUIT FROM THE TREE OF LIFE

He is ready to trade baskets with you right now. He will take your little tiny basket of bad things and give you his big basket of the everlasting fruit of the tree of Life. ''He that spared not his own son, but delivered him up for us all, how shall he not with him give us all things?'' (Rom. 8:32).

CHAPTER 10

SAFE AT LAST

Then shall the dust return to the earth as it was and the spirit shall return unto God who gave it.
(Eccles. 12:7)

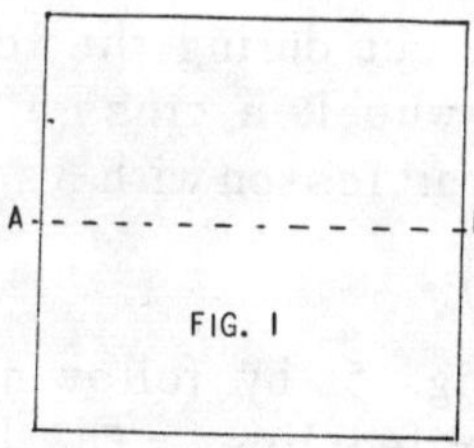

FIG. 1

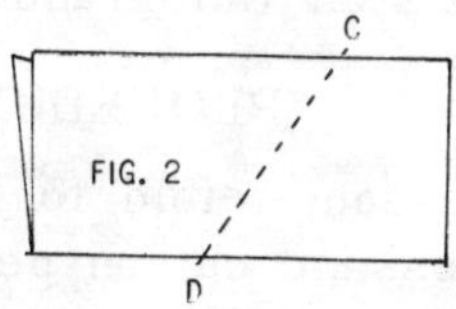

FIG. 2

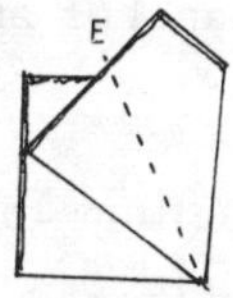

FIG. 3

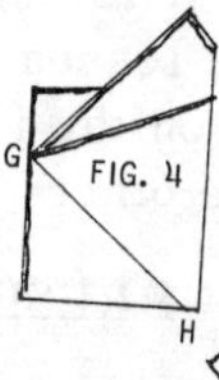

FIG. 4

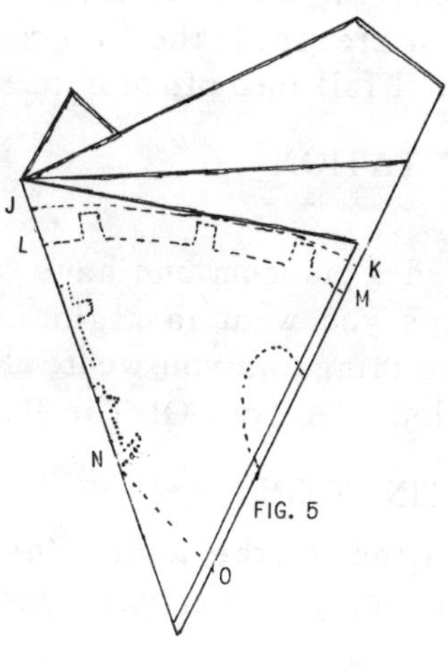

FIG. 5

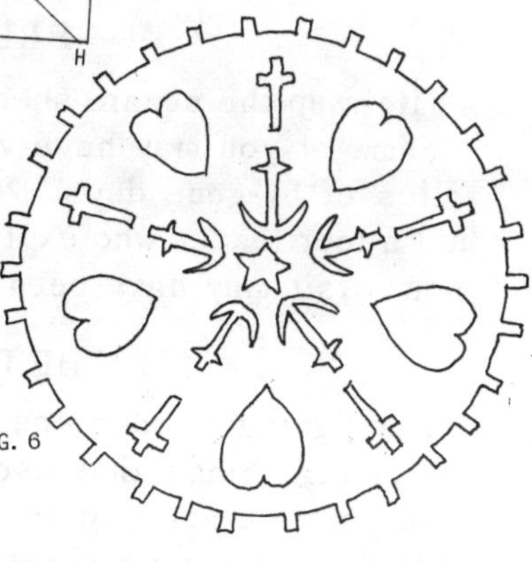
FIG. 6

PROPERTY

A sheet of newsprint 15 X 15 inches in size, pencil and scissors.

PREPARATION

Prefold Fig. 1 on line AB and Fig. 2 on line CD to make Fig. 3. Fold Fig. 3 on line EF and Fig. 4 on line GH. This will make Fig. 5 (enlarged drawing). Mark light pencil lines as shown by dotted lines on Fig. 5. A curved line JK and another line LM, a half cross, a half anchor, and a half heart. Mark a straight line at the lower tip of the object (line ON). When all are cut during the lesson you will have a compass, a pilot wheel, a cross, a heart an anchor and a star. Unfold and start lesson with a square.

PROCEDURE

During the lesson, refold to Fig. 5 by following the prefolded creases and cut on penciled lines. The larger the sheet, the better. It is suggested that since you refold the sheet during the lesson several times that you mark a penciled guide line on the first crease. If the first crease is folded correctly, the others will fall into place naturally.

PRESENTATION

(Hold up the square sheet).

Some of you may have visited a museum and have seen relics of by-gone days. Perhaps you went in a group and had a tour leader who explained things as you went along. Your visit may have been called, "A Tour Of The Past."

1. THE DESTINATION

I am going to take you on a tour of the future. Instead of seeing things that used to be, you are going to see thing that are going to be.

Here is a square sheet of paper that will take you into the future. The Bible speaks of something square. It is a city. Its name is HEAVEN and it is described as The City Foursquare. It is a big city, 1500 miles long, 1500 miles wide and 1500 miles high. It is like a big square, just like the blocks you once played with. Each side is equal because it is foursquare.(Rev. 21:16).

It is the place Jesus has gone to prepare for his family. (John 14:3). If he is your Savior, you are a part of his family and God is your father. You will go there when you die or when Jesus comes again, whichever is first. (1 Thess. 4:17).

2. THE CHARTED COURSE

(Fold Fig. 1 to Fig. 5 and cut on line JK to make a circular object).

To get to this City Foursquare you must make a voyage over the sea of life. To be sure you make a safe voyage you must follow a laid out course of travel. Every ship has something like this (Hold up circle). It is a compass and it shows the steersman or helmsman which direction the ship is traveling in and reminds him when he is getting off the charted course.

God has provided such a compass for you as you travel on the sea of life. It is the Bible or the Word of God. You need to study its pages to check and correct your course. A helmsman who pays no attention to the compass in his pilot's cabin will cause the ship to become a derelect of the deep or will cast his anchor in the wrong harbor.

3. THE HELMSMAN

(Refold to Fig. 5 and cut on line LM so there are three short extensions which will become handles of the wheel when unfolded).

This is an important part of every ship. It is called the "Pilot's Wheel" and with it the ship is steered toward the right harbor.

Of equal importance is the one whose hand is on the wheel. He guides the ship by turning the rudder and corrects the course and avoids the dangerous icebergs and the shallows and the narrows and the ocean graveyards, and finally brings the ship with all of its passengers and cargo to the harbor of the right city.

God has provided such a helmsman on your voyage which began at the cradle and ends at the grave. Jesus is that helmsman and you must have the faith to believe that he knows the way to the Father's house. One time, some of his friends said, "We do not know the way." He answered, "I am the way." (John 14:6). This meant they were to leave everything to him, and that as long as they followed him, he would lead the way, and though the way might be rough and painful and discouraging, he would bring them safely to the right destination.

4. THE REQUEST FOR PASSAGE

(Refold to Fig. 5 and complete the rest of the cuts, the heart, the cross, the star and the anchor. Then unfold and show).

God has provided everything for the voyage, but there are some things he does not do, some things that you yourself must do. (Point to the heart). You must make a decision to get aboard, and do it with all your heart. God has voted for you and the devil has voted against you. Now the vote is tie, and you must cast the deciding vote. God built the heart into the plan of salvation. The heart has nothing to do with providing it, but only in receiving it. There must be action on your part (John 1:12).

You must be ready to ride the rough sea and even suffer seasickness. Seasickness is bad. First you are afraid you are going to die, and then you are afraid you are not going to and wish you could. Not everyone will go to heaven. Some will miss the boat (2 Thess. 3:5, Rom. 10:10).

5. THE TICKET

Some of you may say, "Teacher, I want to go. I am ready to start right now, but I have no money for the ticket." (Point to the cross). The beautiful thing about this voyage is that your passage is already paid for. You just have to get aboard with a happy song and sing, "Nothing in my hand I bring, simply to thy cross I cling." "Forasmuch as ye know that ye were not redeemed with corruptible things, such as silver and gold, but with the precious blood of Christ." (1 Pet. 1:19).

6. THE ASSURANCE

(Point to the star)

The star is at the very center of the chart. It stands for God, the unchanging one,"The same yesterday, today and forever." (Heb 13:8).

The stars are always in place, like the north star, the dipper, etc. No matter what time of the year it is, or what the weather is like, be it hot or cold, stormy or calm, the stars are always in place. Likewise, you can depend on God. He is always there and you can be sure of him. David found that God is always present, in life or in death. (Ps. 139:7-12 and Ps. 23:4).

SAFE AT LAST

(Point to anchor).

The wonders and joys on the other shore of the sea of life will not be wholly known until the anchor is cast in the harbor of heaven. Then shall we know as we are known. (1 Cor. 13:12) (John 1 3:2).

The anchor of a ship is dropped so the ship will not drift away. When you come to the end of the voyage on the other shore of the sea if life, eternity will be for keeps. Your ship will never drift.

There is a free ticket for all who will claim it. Already the great horn of the ship has sounded its departure warning signal, announcing that all who are going must now get aboard. Are you aboard? If not, the gangway is still open and the gangplank is still out. ALL ABOARD!

OTHER LESSONS AVAILABLE

By the same author

The jackets listed below each have 8 visual aids. Each has a surprise climax and is complete with all the objects.

Available through your book store or from the publishers of this book.

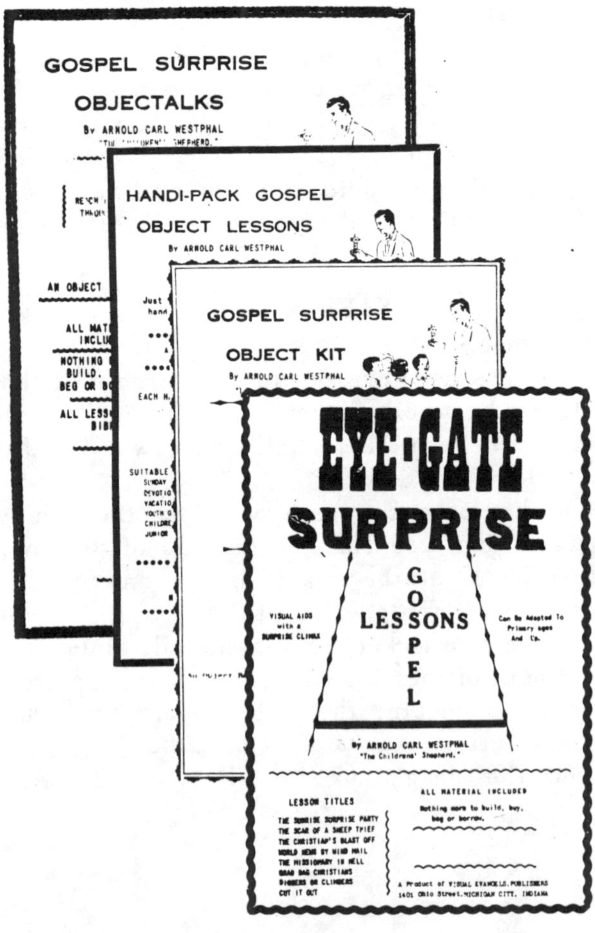

STILL MORE LESSONS AVAILABLE.

Each of the four jackets listed below has 8 lessons. Can be adapted to ages above Primary department.

Excellent for Vacation Schools, department specials, Devotionals, camps, Evangelistic meetings, etc.

ASK YOUR BOOKSTORE OR WRITE THE PUBLISHER OF THIS BOOK.

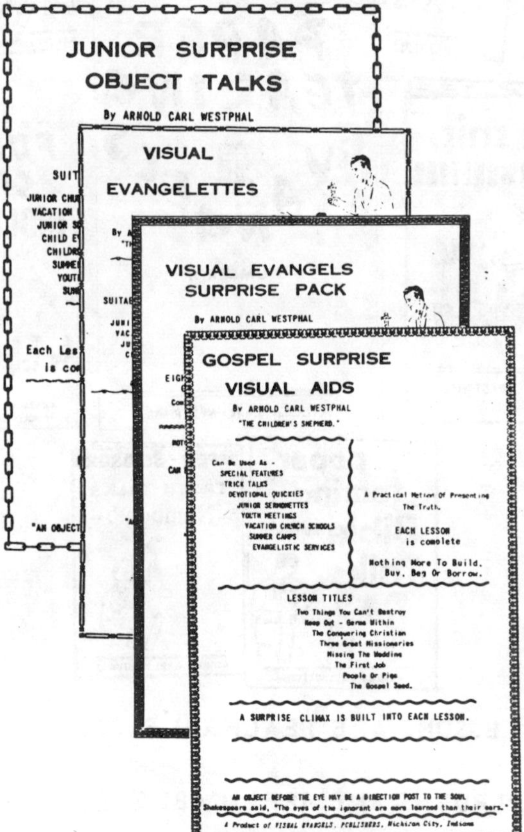

The author has developed 50 Gospel lessons using magic devices, pocket tricks and simple self-contained and easy to do items. No sleight of hand is used. Write to this publisher for lists and prices